Also by Frederick Seidel

LIFE ON EARTH

THE COSMOS POEMS

GOING FAST

MY TOKYO

THESE DAYS

POEMS, 1959–1979

SUNRISE

FINAL SOLUTIONS

AREA CODE 2I2

AREA CODE 212

Frederick Seidel

FARRAR, STRAUS AND GIROUX

NEW YORK

Farrar, Straus and Giroux

19 Union Square West, New York 10003

Copyright © 2002 by Frederick Seidel

Distributed in Canada by Douglas & McIntyre Ltd.

Printed in the United States of America

First edition, 2002

Library of Congress Cataloging-in-Publication Data

Seidel, Frederick, 1936–

Area code 212 / Frederick Seidel.—1st ed.

p. cm.

ISBN 0-374-10581-2 (hc : alk. paper)

1. Manhattan (New York, N.Y.)—Poetry.

I. Title: Area code two one two.   II. Title.

PS3569.E5 A88 2002

811'.54—dc21

2002020119

Designed by Peter A. Andersen

www.fsgbooks.com

1   3   5   7   9   10   8   6   4   2

TO JONATHAN GALASSI

CONTENTS

AREA CODE 212

AREA CODE 212

I DO

I do
Standing still.
I do in my head.
I do everything to keep active.

Everything is excellent.
I do pablum. I do doo-doo. I do heroic deeds.
I do due
Diligence.

I do heroic deeds. I don't move.
I do love
The sky above
Which is black.

I do white gloves at the dances,
But I don't dance with the fascists.
I do beat and smash their stupid wishes.
I take you to be my.

The river is turning into
A place to drown.
The road lay down
In front of the car.

Everything in hell was
Talking English long ago.
I mean English.
I mean fruit bowl. I mean upper crust. I mean, really!

The ocean swings back into view in inland St. Louis.
The time is then.
My headmaster's exotic psychotic wife goes completely
Round the bend and maintains

The Mississippi is down there and up here
Is Berchtesgaden. I am shooting up on this.
Breast milk leaks from the insertion point.
His wife—my bride—wanders around the campus saying I do.

THE BATHROOM DOOR

Decapitated, he looks much the same,
The same homeless mind.
He watches a starving man
Eating his hiccups

Because he has nothing else to eat
In front of the mirror that is
Brushing his teeth.
Then he goes to bed headless. Then

He hears his wife get out of their bed
And lock the bathroom door
That they never lock.
Both of them are drunk.

He sleeps with his eyes shut in the dark
For a few minutes and then he gets up.
But he doesn't get up.
She comes back to bed.

She says I am so afraid.
She says I feel cold.
He asks her what she has done.
He makes her stand up and walk. He calls 911.

He will go to the theater
Of the locking of the bathroom door, hiccup
Click, and how he stayed in bed
For the rest of his life.

He remembers something else.
That he did get up. He stood
Outside the door.
He went back to a bed

Even more terrible than the loyal eyes
Of a dog about to be euthanized.
Than the efforts of a racehorse
Who will have to be shot to rise.

DOWNTOWN

Think of the most disgusting thing you can think of.
It is beautiful in its way.
It has two legs.
It has a head of hair.

It goes downtown.
It goes into an art gallery.
It pulls out a gun.
It kills its friend.

Never mind how much money they made.
Start thinking about what matters.
The MV Agusta motorcycle
Is the most beautiful.

I Do was one.
The Bathroom Door was another.
I Do was one.
Pulled out a gun and fired.

It was point-blank.
It died instantly.
The fragment was Sappho.
You can imagine how beautiful.

The person is walking
Ahead of you on the sidewalk.
You see its back but its face
Is facing you as it walks away.

As if the neck were
Broken, but the face is calm.
The name of the face you
Face is the United Nations.

It is a lovely Picasso walking away
On a broken neck and looking straight ahead back.
First came the seen, then thus the palpable
Elysium, though it were in the halls of hell.

THE SERPENT

Who is this face as little
As a leaf,
The neck a stem?
The furnace waits.

Someone is happening
To someone. Someone is
Alive and enters
Defiantly.

Her lips are full.
The mouth is open.
The living room is full
Of mahogany and art.

The serpent concentrates its gaze until the serpent is
A sumo wrestler agile as a dragonfly,
A furnace eating only good
To stay big.

The girl is a delicate
Drop.
The beautiful face
Is a leaf.

The dragonfly
Practices touch-and-go landings
At the little airport, landing to take off,
See-through with heartbeats.

The serpent is not a serpent
But a lyre.
It asks to play.
It asks the girl to let a dragon fly.

Someone is sailing clay pigeons
And blowing them apart perfectly.
Someone is kissing
The other.

GETAWAY

I think you do
But it frightens you.
I have the guns
In the car.

I wanted to save
Someone and
The rest. It will happen.
I will take you hostage.

Also I wasn't
Going to fall in love
But when you're fleeing
You're flying.

Someone had to take
My blindfold off for me to
Just take off. I turn the key in your ignition.
Contact! The propeller flickers.

We are taking off to
Elope.
Have another
One

For the road. Burn the birth certificates.
Run the roadblock.
All the whirling lights
On the roofs of their cars.

They're going to check
The trunk and find our bodies.
I won't.
We jump out firing.

I am already in you.
I am rafting down your bloodstream.
That is already over.
I have entered.

NOTHING WILL

Root canal is talking
To the opposite —
Twenty-three years old,
With eyes like very dilated

Dewdrops sideways.
Age is visiting
The other side of the moon,
When the moon was young.

Wow, to see the side
That never faces the earth is cool,
And kiss newborn skin
That you could eat off of.

A clean twenty-three-year-old
Heart is tourism
For the senator
Visiting the strange.

You fly there, then get out and walk.
The space shot lands
And he gets out and flies and then on foot.
He is looking at her tits.

The future will not last.
It is coming towards her
On safari
To watch the ancient king of the savannah roar and mate

Despite a root
Canal spang in the middle.
Nothing will.
Not even root canal. Revive his satrapy.

He is rowing down a canal
Of Royal Palms on either side
And the ocean is near. The oil spill is near
Enough for her to hear it greasing the shore.

pH

Phineas has turned
To face the quiet Phoebe to
Touch her cheek.
Phineas, who is tender but not meek,

And certainly is not weak,
Is also not named Phineas.
The name is art.
Phineas turns to touch her tenderly,

But the cab runs over a
Pocked-moon stretch of Brooklyn roadway
And his hand is knocked
Into being a brute.

What is the pH of New York?
PH is
Singing to PH,
Date palm to date palm.

The dunes in every
Direction tower.
Their color is octoroon
In Manhattan at dawn.

That is the color
Of the heart they share
Which is an oasis
Where one can pause

Before going out to die
In the dunes,
Strangling without water
And without a gun

To shoot at night at the stars.
For the moment, they sing.
The saddle has no camel under it.
They know.

VENUS

Venus is getting
Smaller.
Finally, she is
The size of a mouse.

A fully developed young woman
That size
Makes it difficult
To caress her breasts.

The curly wire
To a Secret Service agent's ear
Ends in a plug actually bigger
Than her derrière.

What a magnificent goddess!
And enormous—when
She stands on the back of your hand
With her glorious assets!

Her steatopygous ass
Sticks straight out—a Hottentot harvest moon!
Her breasts are prodigious.
Her ass is steatopygous.

Her head is
Classically small.
Her eyes and her mouth
Are equally oceans and drops from a dropper.

Venus shrank down
To go to Harvard, and got a tiny degree.
Her Junoesque figure
Is the size of a sea horse.

Mr. Universe
Is in love,
But how will he get in?
Venus, goddess, tell him how!

NIGRA SUM

I'm having a certain amount of difficulty
Because I am finding it hard.
It is all uphill.
I wake up tired.

It is downhill from here.
The Emancipation Proclamation won't change that.
Evidently there have been irregularities apparently.
It is time to get out.

I am going to go public with this
Beautiful big breasts and a penis
Military-industrial complex.
I live in the infield with other connoisseurs

Behind the bars of the gate to the circuit,
Sniffing burning racing oil till I'm high.
On the other side of the gate is the start/finish,
And the red meat of the racebikes raving to race.

I'm not from anywhere. I'm from my head.
That's where I didn't grow up
And went to school.
Oh, I am totally vile and beautiful!

A military-industrial complex with soul!
Nigra sum sed formosa.
I am black but comely,
O ye daughters of Jerusalem:

Therefore has the king loved me, and brought me into his
Chambers. For, lo, the winter is past,
The rain is over and gone:
Rise up, my love, my fair one,

And come away.
Tomorrow I set sail for the bottom, never to return.
The master cabin has its own head—which I'm from.
I'm from my head.

RAIN IN HELL

That was the song he found himself singing.
He heard a splash before he hit the concrete.
There was no water in the pool.
He couldn't stop himself in time.

One day, while he was waiting for the light to change,
And suddenly it began to rain,
And all at once the sun came out,
He saw a rainbow of blood.

He was so excited.
Splash.
That he dove off
The diving board without a thought.

There was no water in the pool.
He heard a splash
Just before he hit the concrete.
Gosh—

From good in bed
To as good as dead!
You smell the rain before it comes.
You smell the clean cool pierce the heat.

He has the air-conditioning on
But keeps the car windows open driving back to town.
It is the story of his life.
He smells the rain before it falls.

It was the middle of the night
In 212, the Area Code of love.
The poem he was writing put
Its arms around his neck.

Why write a poem?
There isn't any rain in hell
So why keep opening an umbrella?
That was the song he found himself singing.

DIDO WITH DILDO

The cord delivers electricity
From the wall socket to my mouth
Which I drink.
I want you all to know how much

My hair stands on end.
You will leave me alive.
You will leave me and live.
I hold midnight in my hand.

The town siren sounds because it's
Noon. The sunlight throws spears
Into the waves
And the gulls scream.

You get there.
Something instantly is wrong.
It only seems it's instantly.
It always is

The case that different time zones
Produce
Different midnights.
I hold a new year in my hand.

She stood on her toes to kiss me
Like in the nineteen fifties.
I glued my mucho macho lips to destiny.
I hurl a fireball at the logjam.

I turn on the TV.
I turn the oven off.
I make a call on my cell phone
To the mirror.

I see in the mirror Aeneas
Has changed.
He is drinking vodka odorlessly.
Into Dido wearing a dildo.

JANUARY

I have a dream
And must be fed.
The manta rays when you wade out
Ripple toward your outstretched hand.

The answer is
The friendliness of the body.
There is no answer, but the answer is
The friendliness of the body

Is the stars above
The dock at night.
And in the afternoon lagoon flags lazily flap
Their bodies toward yours

To be fed. I landed on
An atoll in the soft
Perfume.
The airport air was sweet. The blond January breeze was young.

The windchill factor
Which is Western thought
Received an IV drip of syrup of clove.
I have a dream. I have a dream the

Background radiation is a
Warm ocean, and a pasture for
Desire, and a
Beach of royal psalms.

The IV bag is a warm ocean,
Is a body not your own feeding your body.
My body loves your body
Is the motto of Tahiti.

Two flying saucers mating,
One on top the other, flap and flow, in love.
Each is a black
Gun soft as a glove.

FEBRUARY

The best way not to kill yourself
Is to ride a motorcycle very fast.
How to avoid suicide?
Get on and really ride.

Then comes Valentine's Day.
It is February, but very mild.
But the MV Agusta is in storage for the winter.
The Ducati racer is deeply asleep and not dreaming.

Put the pills back in the vial.
Put the gun back in the drawer.
Ventilate the carbon monoxide.
Back away from the railing.

You can't budge from the edge?
You can meet her in front of the museum.
It is closed today—every Monday.
If you are alive, happy Valentine's Day!

All you brave failed suicides, it is a leap year.
Every day is an extra day
To jump. It is February 29th
Deep in the red heart of February 14th.

On the steps in front of the museum,
The wind was blowing hard.
Something was coming.
Winter had been warm and weird.

Hide not thy face from me.
For I have eaten ashes like bread,
And mingled my drink with weeping,
While my motorcycles slept.

She arrives out of breath,
Without a coat, blazing health,
But actually it is a high flu fever that gives her glory.
Life is death.

IN CAP FERRAT

God made human beings so dogs would have companions.
Along the promenade dogs are walking women.
One is wearing fur
Although the day is warm.

The fur
Trots behind a cur.
The mongrel sparkles and smiles
Leading her by the leash.

The month of March, that leads to hell,
Is plentiful in Cap Ferrat.
There is gambling around the bend
In the bay at the Casino in creamy Monte Carlo.

White as the Taj Mahal,
White as that stove of grief,
Is the cloud
Just passing by.

The air is herbs.
The sea is blue chrome curls.
The mutt sparkles and leers
And lifts a leg.

White as the weightless Taj Mahal,
White as the grief and love it was,
The day is warm, the sea is blue.
The dog, part spitz, part spots, is zest

And piss and Groucho Marx
Dragging a lady along.
The comedy
Is raw orison.

Dogs need an owner to belong to.
Dogs almost always die before their owners do.
But one dog built a Taj Mahal for two.
I loved you.

MARCH

He discovered he would have to kill.
He went to Paris to study how.
He returned home to throw out the colonial French.
He never left the United States.

He was a boy who was afraid.
He talked arrogance, secretly sick at heart.
He oozed haughty nonchalance, like a duke sitting on a shooting stick.
He grinned toughness on the playing field running behind his teeth.

He strutted in the school library, smirking
Like Charlie Chaplin twirling his cane jauntily.
He was a genius but he was afraid
He would burst into flames of fame and cry.

This Ho Chi Minh was arrogant. This Ho Chi Minh was shy.
Then he discovered poetry. It was in Florida
One March, at spring break, with his sister and parents,
Having parted for the week from his first girlfriend ever.

He wrote: *The sea pours in while my heart pours out*—
Words to that effect.
Even for age thirteen,
This was pretty dim.

This was the year of his bar mitzvah.
It was his genocidal coming of age in Cambodia.
Everyone who wore glasses was executed.
He took his off.

They killed everything in sight in a red blur.
It rained
A rainbow of the color red.
They wore black pajamas in a red bed.

They killed anyone named Fred.
This to start Utopia. Everyone was dead.
The Algerians blew up the French.
The French horribly tortured them to find out.

EASTER

The wind lifts off his face,
Which flutters
In the wind and snaps back and forth,
Just barely attached.

It smiles horribly—
A flag flapping on a flagpole.
Why is this idiot patriot
Smiling?

He is horribly
In love.
It is embarrassing to see
The red, white and blue.

The field of stars
Is the universe, his mind,
Which thinks about her constantly
And dials her number. *Hello. It's me.*

It really hurts
To see it in his face.
The awful smile of a dog
Is a grimace.

You can believe
In God again—God looks like him.
The Easter koan says the gas tank must be full
But empty. The taut wind sock

Sounds the trumpet,
Summoning all
To the new.
The trumpet sounds!

Sweet is spreading salt,
But only on the ice where people walk,
Only it is rice in slow motion showering fragrant
Spring rain on the couples.

APRIL

A baby elephant is running along the ledge across
The front of an apartment building ten stories up.
What must be the young woman handler desperately gives chase,
Which has a comic aspect as she hangs on by the rope.

But the baby elephant falls, yanking the young woman floatingly
To her death on a ledge lower down.
The baby elephant lies dead on Broadway.
Every year it does.

Birds bathe in the birdbath in the warm blood.
The bed upstairs is red.
The sheets are red.
The pillows are blood.

The baby elephant looks like a mouse running away
Or a cockroach scuttling away on a shelf,
Followed by the comically running sandpiper
Holding the rope.

It is everywhere when you restart your computer.
You don't see it and then you do.
A half has already fallen to the street,
And the other is falling and hits the ledge.

Now is a vase of flowers
Maniacally blooming red.
The medallion cabs seem very yellow
Today—as yellow as lymph.

Every April 1st Frank O'Hara's ghost
Stops in front of the Olivetti showroom
On Fifth Avenue—which hasn't been there for thirty years.
He's there for the Lettera 22 typewriter outside on a marble pedestal

With a supply of paper—to dash off a city poem, an April poem,
That he leaves in the typewriter for the next passerby,
On his way to work at the Museum of Modern Art, because
The baby elephant is running along the ledge, chased by its handler.

MAY

A man picks up a telephone to hear his messages,
Returns the handset to the cradle, looking stunned.
The pigeon on the ledge outside the window
Bobs back and forth in front of New York City, moaning.

A man takes roses to a doctor, to her office,
And gets himself buzzed in, and at the smiling front desk
Won't give his name to the receptionist, just leaves red roses.
The doctor calls the man the next day, leaves a message.

There isn't anything more emptiness than this,
But it's an emptiness that's almost estival.
The show-off-ness of living full of May
Puts everything that's empty on display.

The pigeon on the ledge outside the window
Moans, bobbing up and down, releasing whiteness.
The day releases whiteness on the city.
And May increases.

Seersucker flames of baby blue and white
Beneath a blue-eyed Caucasian sky with clouds
Fill up the emptiness of East Side life
Above a center strip that lets red flowers grow.

They call them cut flowers when they cut them.
They sell the living bodies at the shop.
A man is bringing flowers to a doctor,
But not for her to sew them up.

And May is getting happy, and the temperature is eighty.
And the heart is full of palm trees, even when it's empty.
The center strip migraine down Park Avenue sees red.
Girl with a Red Hat in the Vermeer show is what it sees.

Vermeer went in a day and a half from being healthy to being dead.
A city made of pigeons is moaning in a morgue that's a garden.
The red hat reddens the Metropolitan.
It's its harem.

VENUS WANTS JESUS

Venus wants Jesus.
Jesus wants justice.
That one wants this.
This one wants that.

I want.
It means I lack.
Working men and women on
May 1st march.

They want to increase
The minimum wage and they will form a line.
My fellow glandes march
Entirely

Around the girl while
Around the world bands
Are playing.
On the White House lawn, "Hail to the Chief"

Greets the arriving helicopter slowly curtsying
On the landing pad.
They ought
To wait till the rotor stops. The president

Descends
The stairs waving. Behind him is
The uniformed aide with the attaché case carrying
The codes.

The president
Can place a lei around
A billion necks
In an hour.

They wanted to live till June.
They wanted the time.
They wanted to say goodbye.
They wanted to go to the bathroom before.

MV AGUSTA RALLY,
CASCINA COSTA, ITALY

Each June there is a memorial Mass
For Count Corrado Agusta in the family church,
Whose factory team of overwhelming motorcycles
Won every Grand Prix championship for years.

The courtyard in front of the sinister stark house
Where Corrado was raised blazes with victory.
The charming young choir in the tiny church sings,
To the strumming of a guitar, that other glory story.

In her MV Agusta T-shirt, the reader reads aloud the lesson.
The roaring of a lion about to devour her
Is an MV 500cc GP racer getting revved up for the rally:
The caviar and flower of Grand Prix four-stroke power.

The champions have no idle, so not
To die they have to
Roar. They roar like the lions in the Coliseum.
They roar like a pride of blood-red hearts in the savannah.

Someone blips
The throttle of the three-cylinder
500, one kind of sound, then someone pushes into life
The four. Its bel canto throat catches fire.

The priest elevates the Host
And his bored theatrical eyes,
To melodramatize the text,
Roar.

It's like the Mass they hold in France
To bless the packs of hounds before a hunt.
The choir of hunting horns blares bloodcurdling fanfares
And lordly stags answer from all the forests around.

I stand in the infield with other connoisseurs near tears
Behind the bars of the gate to the track, smelling burning castor oil.
On the other side of the gate is the start/finish line,
And Monica Agusta standing with her back to me, close enough to touch.

XXI

JUNE

Eternal life begins in June.
Her name is fill the name in.
My contubernalis, my tent mate,
My woman in the tent with me in Latin.

The next world is the one I'm in.
My June contubernium.
My tent mate through the whole campaign.
The June moon, burning pure Champagne,

Starts foaming from its tail and rising.
One minute into launch and counting.
The afterlife lifts off like this.
The afterlife begins to blast.

The breathing of my sleeping dog
Inflates the moonlit room with silence.
The afterlife begins this way.
The universe began today.

The afterlife is here on earth.
It's what you're doing when you race
And enter each turn way too fast
And brake as late as possible always.

Of course the world does not exist.
A racebike raving down the straight
Explodes into another world,
Downshifts for the chicane, brakes hard,

And in the other world ignites
The flames of June that burn in hell.
My contubernalis, my tent mate.
My woman in the tent with me does octane.

Ducati racing red I ride,
Ride red instead of wrong or right.
The color red in hell looks cool.
In heaven it's for sex on sight.

XXII

JUNE ALLYSON AND MAE WEST

In the middle
Of the field of vision
Is a hole that is
Surrounded by a woman.

The hole is life.
The ones who are
About to be born
Have no choice.

The hole is life.
The ones who are
About to be born
Have no choice.

In the middle
Of the field stood
The middle of the light
Which is love, a heart of light.

I got better.
I can remember taking
A streetcar.
It was June.

The name of the movie star was June
Allyson who was with me in my hospital room.
I bet the glorious wicked star Mae
West would.

June made Mae good.
Mae made June bad.
Is it bearable?
The situation is

No one ever gets well.
People can't
Even stand up.
They pay to cry.

XXIII

JULY

Phineas is crossing the Pont des Arts,
But he is doing it in New York.
He has made up the Phineas part.
That is not his name.

Nothing is.
Nothing is his.
He is living in Paris,
On Broadway.

Two minutes from his door
Is the Pont des Arts arcing
Over the Seine.
Bateaux mouches like bugs of light

Slide by at night under his feet, fading away in English.
Shock waves vee against the quais.
Mesdames and gentlemen, soon we have Notre-Dame.
The letter *P* is walking across the Pont des Arts.

Back in New York,
Except he *is* in New York,
He is in Paris.
He strolls home to the rue de Seine, punches in the code and goes in.

The next morning the streets
Are bleeding under his feet.
They are cleaning themselves.
Apparently, they are not that young.

The trees are green.
In the Jardin du Luxembourg he says her name.
He watches the children riding the donkeys on the red dirt.
An adult holds the halter and walks alongside.

One tree is vomiting and sobbing
Flowers.
The smell is powerful.
How quatorze July it is to be a donkey and child.

XXIV

HUGH JEREMY CHISHOLM

With Jeremy Chisholm at the Lobster Inn on our way to Sagaponack,
Eating out on the porch in the heat, flicking cigarettes into the inlet.
We ate from the sea and washed it down with Chablis,
Punctuated by our unfiltered Camels, in our eternal July.

Billy Hitchcock landed his helicopter at a busy gas station
In Southampton July 4th weekend, descended from the sky like a god
To buy a candy bar from the vending machine outside,
Unwrapped the candy bar and flew away, rotors beating.

Chisholm found a jeweler to paint his Tank Watch black.
It had been his father's, one of the first Cartier made.
The gold case in blackface was sacrilege.
Chisholm wore it like a wrist corsage.

In a helicopter that belonged to the Farkas family,
The carpet of cemeteries seemed endless choppering out to J.F.K.
So much death to overfly! It could take a lifetime.
They were running out of cemeteries to be dead in.

Hovering at fifteen feet,
Waiting for instructions on where to land,
Told to go elsewhere,
We heeled over and flew very low, at the altitude of a dream.

Bessie Cuevas had introduced me to this *fin de race* exquisite
Who roared around town in his souped-up Mini-Minor,
Who poured Irish whiskey on his Irish oatmeal for breakfast,
Who was as beautiful as the young Prince Yusupov

Who had used his wife as bait to kill Rasputin and, later in Paris,
Always in makeup, was a pal of the Marquis de Cuevas, Bessie's dad.
Yusupov dressed up a pet ape in chauffeur's livery
And drove down the Champs-Élysées with the ape behind the wheel.

WASPs can't get lung cancer smoking Camels,
Chisholm said, taking the usual long deep drag—look at cowboys!
That July they found a tumor
As big as the Ritz inoperably near his heart.

XXV

AUGUST

Sky-blue eyes,
A bolt of lightning drinking
Skyy vodka,
A demon not afraid of happiness,

Asks me about my love life here in hell.
I lunge at what I understand I belong to.
I flee, too.
It's her fate. It's too late.

I see the sky from a couch at the Carlyle.
Blond is dressed in black.
It all comes back.
The sky is black.

Thunder violently shakes
The thing it holds in its teeth
Until it snaps the neck
And rain pours down in release and relief,

Releasing paradise,
The smell of honeysuckle and of not afraid of happiness.
Lightning flashes once
To get the sky eyes used to it,

And then flashes again
To take the photograph.
The blackout startled her and started it.
Lightning flickers in Intensive Care.

I am speaking in Ecstatic.
The couch is floating on the carpet.
The waiter burns
From all the discharge and surge, and brings more drinks.

Coition is divine human
Rebirth and ruin having drinks in a monsoon,
In the upholstered gallery outside the bar, in the gold light.
The Prince of Darkness dipped in gold is God.

XXVI

SEPTEMBER

The woman is so refined.
The idea of refinement gets redefined.
Doing it with her is absurd.
Like feeding steak to a hummingbird.

Her hair colorist colored her hair gold
To give her a look. It made her look cold.
Her face suddenly seemed see-through like a breath
In a bonnet of gold and she was in a casket and it was death.

She looked more beautiful than life.
She said she wanted to be my wife.
She comes with a psychiatrist to maintain her.
She comes with a personal trainer.

The September trees are still green in Central Park
Until they turn black after dark.
The apartments in the buildings turn their lamps on.
And then the curtains are drawn.

One person on a low floor pulls the curtain back and stares out,
But pulls the curtain closed again when there's a shout,
Audible on Fifth Avenue, from inside the park.
Somewhere a dog begins to bark.

I climb into the casket of this New York night.
I climb into the casket of the curtained light.
I climb into the casket and the satin.
I climb into the casket to do that in.

Into her roaring arms, wings of a hummingbird,
A roar of wings without a word,
A woman looking up at me and me looking down
Into the casket at the town.

I see down there His Honor the Mayor
In St. Patrick's Cathedral, head bowed in prayer.
His friend—wings roaring—hovers beside him in the pew.
Death is all there is. Death will have to do.

XXVII

THE TENTH MONTH

Someone is wagging a finger in her face—*Charlotte!*
Down here in hell we don't do that!
As if she were a child. Charlotte has arrived
To test the torture.

This is a test. This is only a test. Charlotte
Is yelling at Charlotte for a violation.
Charlotte, as a Human Rights Watch
Observer of sorts, has descended from heaven to an early fall.

Oh dear, is it really October?
Is Charlotte really nearly over?
She still says actress—most actresses today would call themselves
An actor. A star walks down upper Broadway being beautiful

With her famous eyes. *Hello from hell,*
She tells her cell phone.
She's ready to hand
Down the indictments and waves her wand.

The crimes sparkle in the moonlight.
Actually, it's rather wonderful to stalk
The Upper West Side midday,
Between the Hudson River and Central Park,

Looking for a self to put the handcuffs on.
It's lovely if there's been a human rights violation.
There's also cruelty to animals,
The child pornography of do-gooders.

The animal is strapped down for the vivisection, conscious,
Buying a book in Barnes & Noble, pursued by fans
Telling her they love her movies here in hell,
And would she do it to herself for them again.

A man comes to the tenth month of the year and calls it Charlotte—
I don't believe in anything, I do
Believe in you. You always play
A garter-belted corpse of someone young.

XXVIII

FALL

It is
A hole surrounded
By a voluptuous
Migraine.

It was a universe that could
Burst out
And start
Without a trace

Of where it came from.
The background radiation
Is what's
Left of

The outburst at the start.
The background radiation
Is the delicious
Migraine. The hole of life

Is about to
Start.
Don't make sense.
It is about to start again.

Umbrellas pop open.
Mushroom caps approach a newsstand.
The trees wear truth and rouge.
The trees start to sing

In the soft.
The old penis smells food
And salivates.
One hundred ninety horsepower at

The crank
Going two hundred miles an hour down the straight
Is another motorcycle death
From Viagra in October.

XXIX

OCTOBER

It is time to lose your life,
Even if it isn't over.
It is time to say goodbye and try to die.
It is October.

The mellow cello
Allée of trees is almost lost in sweetness and mist
When you take off your watch at sunrise
To lose your life.

You catch the plane.
You land again.
You arrive in the place.
You speak the language.

You will live in a new house,
Even if it is old.
You will live with a new wife,
Even if she is too young.

Your slender new husband will love you.
He will walk the dog in the cold.
He will cook a meal on the stove.
He will bring you your medications in bed.

Dawn at the city flower market downtown.
The vendors have just opened.
The flowers are so fresh.
The restaurants are there to decorate their tables.

Your husband rollerblades past, whizzing,
Making a whirring sound, winged like an angel—
But stops and spins around and skates back
To buy some cut flowers in the early morning frost.

I am buying them for you.
I am buying them for your blond hair at dawn.
I am buying them for your beautiful breasts.
I am buying them for your beautiful heart.

XXX

NOVEMBER

I've never been older.
It doesn't.
I can't explain.
Every November is one more.

I've used up my amount.
I've nearly run out.
I'm out of penis.
I've run out.

I look out the spaceship's vast
Expense of greenhouse glass
At the stars.
It will take a million years.

You open your head.
You look in the dictionary.
You look it up.
You look at the opposite.

You open the violin case.
You take it out.
Actually, it is a viola.
Actually, it is November.

You grab the handrails with the
Treadmill speeding up.
Oh my God. Don't stop.
It is possible that

The president traveling in an open limousine
Has been shot.
My fellow Americans, ask not
What your country can do for you in

November. The doorman
Holds the door.
The taxi
Without a driver pulls up.

XXXI

GOD EXPLODING

They all claim responsibility for inventing God,
Including the ruthless suicides who call themselves God Exploding.
All the rival groups, of course, immediately take credit
For terrorist atrocities they did not commit.

One of the terrorist acts they did not commit
Was inventing rock 'n' roll, but, hey,
The birth of Elvis/Jesus is as absolute as the temperature
Of the background radiation, 4°K.

1, 2, 3, 4—I sing of a maiden that is makeles.
King of alle kinges to here sone che ches.
He cam also stille
Ther his moder was,

As dew in Aprille that fallith on the gras.
He cam also stille to his moderes bowr
As dew in Aprille that fallith on the flowr.
He cam also stille

There his moder lay,
As dew in Aprille that fallith on the spray.
Moder and maiden
Was never non but che;

Wel may swich a lady Godes moder be.
I hate seeing the anus of a beautiful woman.
I should not be looking. It should not be there.
It started in darkness and ended up a star.

Jewish stars on the L.A. freeway in Jewish cars
Take the off-ramp to the manger
Somewhere in the fields of Harlem,
Bearing gifts of gold and frankincense and myrrh.

Rock 'n' roll in front of the Wailing Wall and weep.
With the stump where your hand was blown off beat your chest.
Hutu rebel soldiers crucify the mountain gorillas.
Hodie Christus natus est.

XXXII

THE WAR OF THE WORLDS

The child stands at the window, after his birthday party,
Gray flannel little boy shorts, shirt with an Eton collar,
St. Louis, Missouri, sixty years ago,
And sees the World Trade Center towers falling.

The window is the wall
The wide world presents to prepubescence.
People on fire are jumping from the eightieth floor
To flee the fireball.

In the airplane blind-dating the south tower,
People are screaming with horror.
The airplane meeting the north tower
Erupts with ketchup.

The window is a wall
Through which the aquarium visitors can see.
Airplanes are swimming
Up to the towers of steel.

Up to the Twin Towers to feed.
People rather than die prefer to leap
From the eightieth floor to their death.
The man stands at his childhood window saving them.

Old enough to undress himself,
Gray flannel little boy shorts, shirt with an Eton collar,
He stands at the worldwide window, after the birthday party,
And sees the mountains collapsing and collapsing.

On the other side of the aquarium glass is September 11th.
Under his birthday party clothes is his underwear and the underwater.
Why bother to wash your clothes, or your skin, why bother to wash,
When you will only get dirty again?

Why bother to live when you will die?
Visitors are peering through the thick glass and taking photographs
Of ground zero—of Allah akbar in formaldehyde in a jar.
God is great. Love is hate.

XXXIII

DECEMBER

I don't believe in anything, I do
Believe in you.
Down here in hell we do don't.
I can't think of anything I won't.

I amputate your feet and I walk.
I excise your tongue and I talk.
You make me fly through the black sky.
I will kill you until I die.

Thank God for you, God.
I do.
My God, it is almost always Christmas Eve this time of year, too.
Then I began to pray.

I don't believe in anything anyway.
I did what I do. I do believe in you.
Down here in hell they do don't.
I can't think of anything we won't.

How beautiful thy feet with shoes.
Struggling barefoot over dunes of snow forever, more falling, forever, Jews
Imagine mounds of breasts stretching to the horizon.
We send them to their breast, mouthful of orison.

I like the color of the smell. I like the odor of spoiled meat.
I like how gangrene transubstantiates warm firm flesh into rotten sleet.
When the blue blackens and they amputate, I fly.
I am flying a Concorde of modern passengers to gangrene in the sky.

I am flying to Area Code 212
To stab a Concorde into you,
To plunge a sword into the gangrene.
This is a poem about a sword of kerosene.

This is my 21st century in hell.
I stab the sword into the smell.
I am the sword of sunrise flying into Area Code 212
To flense the people in the buildings, and the buildings, into dew.

Ray Sokolov commissioned a calendar of nearly two years of monthly poems from me for the Leisure & Arts page of *The Wall Street Journal*. Many of the poems in this book first appeared there, though sometimes under other titles and, in a few cases, with differences in the text. —F.S.